MOTIVATIONAL STORIES COLOR

MR VIVEK KUMAR PANDEY SHAMBHUNATH

ISBN 979-888569260-1

Disclaimer : Disclaimer : During Writing This Book No character & No religious , No Relation Members Are Harmed. It's Only For Study & Entertainment Purpose. Do Not Take Seriously,Written By Mr Vivek Kumar Pandey.

Contents

Contents

Foreword

In This Book There Is 30+ Motivational Stories In English Language. Motivational Word Can Change Your Life 100% Guarantee.What Do In Life ? How Faced The Problem With Quotes.During Writing This Book No Character And No Religion Are Harmed. It's Only For Study Purpose. Written By Mr Vivek Kumar Pandey. winner youngest writer award 1st rank in india 2020.He is only one writer can publish 830 + own book that was greatest successfull in his life.This All Credit Goes To My Super Hero Daddy. This book fully colour Edition.

Preface

Author biography in English :MY NAME IS VIVEK KUMAR PANDEY . I WAS BORN IN 30 SEP 2002,I AM FROM SURAT GUJARAT INDIA.MY DREAM WAS TO BE GOOD WRITERS ,MY FAMILY SUPPORTED ME TO SUCCESSFUL AND I CAN DO IT MY SELF.How do I write? That is a question, I believe, that can be honestly answered by me."CELEBRATING YOUNGEST WRITER AWARD WINNER IN GUJARAT 1ST RANK" MR PANDEY JI . I may think I did a good job writing something . The reader is the one who decides the quality of my writing. I do find writing to be natural to me and therefore find it to be a real challenge. My trick as a challenged writer is to do the best I can and know that I am happy with the final outcome. It may take a while to do my best and there may be quite a few problems I run into along the way.

I am not a greedy person those who are thinking about me and my self I never tried it anyone people suffering from sadness ,I trying to get promoted people suffering from happiness and joy in your Life Time. Now in current situation in India and also world people are unemployed and have no many but our indian governor help to people to get free food from ration card , i also take part in leadership team ,i am Motivational speaker , Film script writer. There was my two dream firstly writer and secondly actor & also my own film is upcoming soon i done almost completely completed script for my film .I AM GOING TO SAY WORD OF HEART TOUCH OUT PLEASE READ IT" , firstly i thanks my father he supports me in this field they always getting inspired me by own his words and behavior ,they always said that he was a biggest person in the world in future and also they purchase fruit and chocolate for me in anytime & anyway , firstly my father buy him then call me Vivek you want a chocolate i will say yes papa but how many tell me ,papa: you tell me how much i buy him i told 1 or 2 chocolate but my father purchase whole the boxes of chocolate and they get suprised me. MY FATHER WAS BORN IN " 20 SEPTEMBER" 1971 IN INDIA.

1) MY FATHER FAVORITE CLOTHES IS KURTA PAIJMA AND ALSO STYLES SHOE

2) FAVORITE SINGER IS KISHORE DA

3) FAVORITE STATE GUJARAT AND KOLKATA , HIS VILLAGE IN BIHAR

4) FAVORITE COLOR BLACK AND WHITE

THEY ALSO LOVE cricket like IPL and one day t-20 .they also like watching a News daily and heard the song daily ,they also interested in tik tok video but in current time tik tok is banned in india but also few videos are in you tube. In lockdown time my family and me very enjoy day daily. my father play daily ludo with his sister and son, daughter.they always loved tea and coffee anytime call me "। विविेक थोडा़ चाय बनाओना विविेक तुम्हारे हाथ का चाय अच्छा लगता है". I make it tea for my father but some reason after the April to june they are suffering from fever and cough , weakness on 6 June 2020 my father death. they not told me say bye bye his life. After death of 6 June on 10 june my mom and dad anniversary.but my father is Best in the world they can do anything for me please take care of father and respect it of your parents.

CHAPTER ONE

Ch : 1 The Dreaming Priest

- Ch : 1 The Dreaming Priest

These motivational stories will encourage you to follow your dreams, treat others with kindness, and never give up on yourself.

Long time ago there lived a priest who was extremely lazy and poor at the same time. He did not want to do any hard work but used to dream of being rich one day. He got his food by begging for alms. One morning he got a pot of milk as part of the alms. He was extremely delighted and went home with the pot of milk. He boiled the milk, drank some of it and put the remaining milk in a pot. He added slight curds in the pot for converting the milk to curd. He then lay down to sleep.

Soon he started imagining about the pot of curd while he lay asleep. He dreamed that if he could become rich somehow all his miseries would be gone. His thoughts turned to the pot of milk he had set to form curd. He dreamed on; "By morning the pot of milk would set, it would be converted to curd. I would churn the curd and make butter from it. I would heat the butter and make ghee out of it. I will then go to that market and sell that ghee, and make some money. With that money i will buy a hen. The hen will lay may eggs which will hatch and there will be many chicken. These chicken will in turn lay hundreds of eggs and I will soon have a poultry farm of my own." He kept on imagining.

"I will sell all the hens of my poultry and buy some cows, and open a milk dairy. All the town people will buy milk from me. I will be very rich and soon I shall buy jewels. The king will buy all the jewels from me. I will be so rich that I will be able to marry an exceptionally beautiful girl from a rich family. Soon I will have a handsome son. If he does any mischief I will be very angry and to teach him a lesson, I will hit him with a big stick."During this dream, he involuntarily picked up the stick next to his bed and thinking that he was beating his son, raised the stick and hit the pot. The pot of milk broke and he awoke from his day dream.

Moral: There is no substitute for hard work. Dreams cannot be fulfilled without hard work.

CHAPTER TWO

Ch : 2 Boy's Job Appraisal

- Ch : 2 Boy's Job Appraisal

A little boy went into a drug store, reached for a soda carton and pulled it over to the telephone. He climbed onto the carton so that he could reach the buttons on the phone and proceeded to punch in seven digits (phone numbers). The store-owner observed and listened to the conversation.

Boy: 'Lady, Can you give me the job of cutting your lawn?

Woman: (at the other end of the phone line): 'I already have someone to cut my lawn.'

Boy: 'Lady, I will cut your lawn for half the price of the person who cuts your lawn now.'

Woman: I'm very satisfied with the person who is presently cutting my lawn.

Boy: (with more perseverance) : 'Lady, I'll even sweep your curb and your sidewalk, so on Sunday you will have the prettiest lawn in all of Palm beach , Florida.'

Woman: No, thank you.

With a smile on his face, the little boy replaced the receiver. The store-owner, who was listening to all this, walked over to the boy.

Store Owner: 'Son... I like your attitude; I like that positive spirit and would like to offer you a job.'

Boy: 'No thanks.'

Store Owner: But you were really pleading for one.

Boy: No Sir, I was just checking my performance at the Job I already have. I am the one who is working for that lady I was talking to!'

Moral: This is what we call 'Self Appraisal'. Every time if we don't get ahead of others, we blame others for it. We should look to our self and compare, find own weaknesses and work hard to throw away weaknesses. Always Work Hard, Honest and with full Dedication. It will always pay up.

CHAPTER THREE

Ch : 3 Keep Your Dream

- Ch : 3 Keep Your Dream

I have a friend named Monty Roberts who owns a horse ranch in San Isidro. He has let me use his house to put on fund-raising events to raise money for youth at risk programs.

The last time I was there he introduced me by saying, "I want to tell you why I let Jack use my horse. It all goes back to a story about a young man who was the son of an itinerant horse trainer who would go from stable to stable, race track to race track, farm to farm and ranch to ranch, training horses. As a result, the boy's high school career was continually interrupted. When he was a senior, he was asked to write a paper about what he wanted to be and do when he grew up.

"That night he wrote a seven-page paper describing his goal of someday owning a horse ranch. He wrote about his dream in great detail and he even drew a diagram of a 200-acre ranch, showing the location of all the buildings, the stables and the track. Then he drew a detailed floor plan for a 4,000-square-foot house that would sit on a 200-acre dream ranch.

"He put a great deal of his heart into the project and the next day he handed it in to his teacher. Two days later he received his paper back. On the front page was a large red F with a note that read, `See me after class.'

"The boy with the dream went to see the teacher after class and asked, `Why did I receive an F?'

"The teacher said, `This is an unrealistic dream for a young boy like you. You have no money. You come from an itinerant family. You have no resources. Owning a horse ranch requires a lot of money. You have to buy the land. You have to pay for the original breeding stock and later you'll have to pay large stud fees. There's no way you could ever do it.' Then the teacher added, `If you will rewrite this paper with a more realistic goal, I will reconsider your grade.'

"The boy went home and thought about it long and hard. He asked his father what he should do. His father said, `Look, son, you have to make up your own mind on this. However, I think it is a very important decision for you.' "Finally, after sitting with it for a week, the boy turned in the same paper, making no changes at all.

He stated, "You can keep the F and I'll keep my dream."

Monty then turned to the assembled group and said, "I tell you this story because you are sitting in my 4,000-square-foot house in the middle of my 200-acre horse ranch. I still have that school paper framed over the fireplace." He added, "The best part of the story is that two summers ago that same schoolteacher brought 30 kids to camp out on my ranch for a week." When the teacher was leaving, he said, "Look, Monty, I can tell you this now. When I was your teacher, I was something of a dream stealer. During those years I stole a lot of kids' dreams. Fortunately you had enough gumption not to give up on yours."

Moral: Don't let anyone steal your dreams. Follow your heart, no matter what. No Dream is too big or too small when one works hard to live it. One should always try making dreams come true no matter what.

CHAPTER FOUR

Ch : 4 Lazy Donkey

- Ch : 4 Lazy Donkey

Bhola owns a donkey called Khandya. Bhola is a very tolerant and kind master. The donkey is lazy and is always finding ways to avoid work.

Once while returning with loads of salt on his back, Khandya falls in the river. He realizes that the fall has lessened the weights of the sacks as the salt has dissolved in the water.

The next few days Khandya purposely falls into the water everyday. Bhola is unhappy at the way Khandya is behaving because he is losing money in the process. He decides to teach Khandya a lesson.

The next day instead of salt bags he loads Khandya with bags of cotton. Khandya is unaware of the change. As planned, he falls into the water and gets the bags wet. He is surprised to find the load unbearable. His otherwise master also starts beating him.

Khandya learns his lesson and starts behaving..

Moral: Work with honesty and sincerity because laziness will ruin you.

CHAPTER FIVE

Ch : 5 Looking at Mirror

- Ch : 5 Looking at Mirror

One day all the employees reached the office and they saw a big advice on the door on which it was written: "Yesterday the person who has been hindering your growth in this company passed away. We invite you to join the funeral in the room that has been prepared in the gym". In the beginning, they all got sad for the death of one of their colleagues, but after a while they started getting curious to know who was that man who hindered the growth of his colleagues and the company itself.

The excitement in the gym was such that security agents were ordered to control the crowd within the room. The more people reached the coffin, the more the excitement heated up. Everyone thought: "Who is this guy who was hindering my progress? Well, at least he died!" One by one the thrilled employees got closer to the coffin, and when they looked inside it they suddenly became speechless. They stood nearby the coffin, shocked and in silence, as if someone had touched the deepest part of their soul. There was a mirror inside the coffin: everyone who looked inside it could see himself.

There was also a sign next to the mirror that said: "There is only one person who is capable to set limits to your growth: it is YOU." You are the only person who can revolutionize your life. You are the only person who can influence your happiness, your realization and your success. You are the only person who can help yourself. Your life does not change when your boss changes, when your friends change, when your partner changes, when your company changes. Your life changes when YOU change, when you go beyond your limiting beliefs, when you realize that you are the only one responsible for your life. "The most important relationship you can have is the one you have with yourself" .

Moral: The world is like a mirror: it gives back to anyone the reflection of the thoughts in which one has strongly believed. The world and your reality are like mirrors lying in a coffin, which show to any individual the death of his divine capability to imagine and create his happiness and his success. It's the way you face Life that makes the difference.

CHAPTER SIX

Ch : 6 Never to Give Up

- Ch : 6 Never to Give Up

One day a farmer's donkey fell down into a well. The animal cried piteously for hours as the farmer tried to figure out what to do. Finally he decided the animal was old and the well needed to be covered up anyway it just wasn't worth it to retrieve the donkey. He invited all his neighbors to come over and help him. They all grabbed a shovel and begin to shovel dirt into the well.

At first, the donkey realized what was happening and cried horribly. Then, to everyone's amazement he quieted down. A few shovel loads later, the farmer finally looked down the well and was astonished at what he saw. With every shovel of dirt that fell on his back, the donkey was doing some thing amazing. He would shake it off and take a step up. As the farmer's neighbors continued to shovel dirt on top of the animal, he would shake it off and take a step up.

Pretty soon, everyone was amazed as the donkey stepped up over the edge of the well and totted off!

Moral: Life is going to shovel dirt on you, all kinds of dirt. The trick is too not to get bogged down by it. We can get out of the deepest wells by not stopping. And by never giving up! Shake it off and take a step up!

CHAPTER SEVEN

Ch : 7 Struggles of our Life

Ch : 7 Struggles of our Life

Once upon a time a daughter complained to her father that her life was miserable and that she didn't know how she was going to make it. She was tired of fighting and struggling all the time. It seemed just as one problem was solved, another one soon followed. Her father, a chef, took her to the kitchen. He filled three pots with water and placed each on a high fire.

Once the three pots began to boil, he placed potatoes in one pot, eggs in the second pot and ground coffee beans in the third pot. He then let them sit and boil, without saying a word to his daughter. The daughter, moaned and impatiently waited, wondering what he was doing. After twenty minutes he turned off the burners. He took the potatoes out of the pot and placed them in a bowl. He pulled the eggs out and placed them in a bowl. He then ladled the coffee out and placed it in a cup.

Turning to her, he asked. "Daughter, what do you see?" "Potatoes, eggs and coffee," she hastily replied.

"Look closer", he said, "and touch the potatoes." She did and noted that they were soft.

He then asked her to take an egg and break it. After pulling off the shell, she observed the hard-boiled egg.

Finally, he asked her to sip the coffee. Its rich aroma brought a smile to her face.

"Father, what does this mean?" she asked.

He then explained that the potatoes, the eggs and coffee beans had each faced the same adversity-the boiling water. However, each one reacted differently. The potato went in strong, hard and unrelenting, but in boiling water, it became soft and weak. The egg was fragile, with the thin outer shell protecting its liquid interior until it was put in the boiling water. Then the inside of the egg became hard. However, the ground coffee beans were unique. After they were exposed to the boiling water, they changed the water and created something new.

"Which one are you?" he asked his daughter. "When adversity knocks on your door, how do you respond? Are you a potato, an egg, or a coffee bean?"

Moral: In life, things happen around us, things happen to us, but the only thing that truly matters is how you choose to react to it and what you make out of it. Life is all about leaning, adopting and converting all the struggles that we experience into something positive.

CHAPTER EIGHT

Ch : 8 The Cracked Pot

- Ch : 8 The Cracked Pot

"A water bearer in India had two large pots, each hung on each end of a pole which he carried across his neck. One of the pots had a crack in it, and while the other pot was perfect and always delivered a full portion of water at the end of the long walk from the stream to the master's house, the cracked pot arrived only half full.

For a full two years this went on daily, with the bearer delivering only one and a half pots full of water in his master's house. Of course, the perfect pot was proud of its accomplishments, perfect to the end for which it was made. But the poor cracked pot was ashamed of its own imperfection, and miserable that it was able to accomplish only half of what it had been made to do.

After two years of what it perceived to be a bitter failure, it spoke to the water bearer one day by the stream. "I am ashamed of myself, and I want to apologize to you. "Why?" asked the bearer. "What are you ashamed of?" "I have been able, for these past two years, to deliver only half my load because this crack in my side causes water to leak out all the way back to your master's house. Because of my flaws, you have to do all of this work, and you don't get full value from your efforts," the pot said.

The water bearer felt sorry for the old cracked pot, and in his compassion he said, "As we return to the master's house, I want you to notice the beautiful flowers along the path." Indeed, as they went up the hill, the old cracked pot took notice of the sun warming the beautiful wild flowers on the side of the path, and this cheered it somewhat. But at the end of the trail, it still felt bad because it had leaked out half its load, and so again it apologized to the bearer for its failure.

The bearer said to the pot, "Did you notice that there were flowers only on your side of your path, but not on the other pot's side? That's because I have always known about your flaw, and I took advantage of it. I planted flower seeds on your side of the path, and every day while we walk back from the stream, you've watered them. For two years I have been able to pick these beautiful flowers to decorate my master's table. Without you being just the way you are, he would not have this beauty to grace his house."

Moral: Each of us has our own unique flaws. We're all cracked pots. In this world, nothing goes to waste. You may think like the cracked pot that you are inefficient or useless in certain areas of your life, but somehow these flaws can turn out to be a blessing in disguise."

CHAPTER NINE

Ch : 9 The Thirsty Crow

- Ch : 9 The Thirsty Crow

One hot day, a thirsty crow flew all over the fields looking for water. For a long time, he could not find any. He felt very weak, almost lost all hope. Suddenly, he saw a water jug below the tree. He flew straight down to see if there was any water inside. Yes, he could see some water inside the jug!

The crow tried to push his head into the jug. Sadly, he found that the neck of the jug was too narrow. Then he tried to push the jug to tilt for the water to flow out but the jug was too heavy.

The crow thought hard for a while. Then looking around it, he saw some pebbles. he suddenly had a good idea. he started picking up the pebbles one by one, dropping each into the jug. As more and more pebbles filled the jug, the water level kept rising. Soon it was high enough for the crow to drink. His plan had worked!

Moral: Think and work hard, you may find solution to any problem.

CHAPTER TEN

Ch : 10 The Travelers and The Plane Tree

- Ch : 10 The Travelers and The Plane Tree

Two men were walking along one summer day. Soon it became too hot to go any further and, seeing a large plane tree nearby, they threw themselves on the ground to rest in its shade. Gazing up into the branches one man said to the other,

"What a useless tree this is. It does not have fruit or nuts that we can eat and we cannot even use its wood for anything."

"Don't be so ungrateful," rustled the tree in reply. "I am being extremely useful to you at this very moment, shielding you from the hot sun. And you call me a good-for-nothing!"

Moral: All of God's creations have a good purpose. We should never belittle God's blessings.

CHAPTER ELEVEN

Ch : 11 Two Frogs

- Ch : 11 Two Frogs

A group of frogs were traveling through the woods, and two of them fell into a deep pit. When the other frogs saw how deep the pit was, they told the two frogs that they were as good as dead. The two frogs ignored the comments and tried to jump up out of the pit with all their might. The other frogs kept telling them to stop, that they were as good as dead. Finally, one of the frogs took heed to what the other frogs were saying and gave up. He fell down and died.

The other frog continued to jump as hard as he could. Once again, the crowd of frogs yelled at him to stop the pain and just die. He jumped even harder and finally made it out. When he got out, the other frogs said, "Did you not hear us?" The frog explained to them that he was deaf. He thought they were encouraging him the entire time.

Moral: There is power of life and death in the tongue. An encouraging word to someone who is down can lift them up and help them make it through the day. So be careful of what you say. Speak life to those who cross your path. The power of words... it is sometimes hard to understand that an encouraging word can go such a long way.

CHAPTER TWELVE

Ch : 12 The Wise Man

- Ch : 12 The Wise Man:

People have been coming to the wise man, complaining about the same problems every time. One day he told them a joke and everyone roared in laughter.

After a couple of minutes, he told them the same joke and only a few of them smiled.

When he told the same joke for the third time no one laughed anymore.

The wise man smiled and said:

“You can’t laugh at the same joke over and over. So why are you always crying about the same problem?”

Moral: Worrying won’t solve your problems, it’ll just waste your time and energy.

CHAPTER THIRTEEN

Ch : 13 An Old Man Lived in the Village

- Ch : 13 An Old Man Lived in the Village:

An old man lived in the village. He was one of the most unfortunate people in the world. The whole village was tired of him; he was always gloomy, he constantly complained and was always in a bad mood.

The longer he lived, the more bile he was becoming and the more poisonous were his words. People avoided him, because his misfortune became contagious. It was even unnatural and insulting to be happy next to him.

He created the feeling of unhappiness in others.

But one day, when he turned eighty years old, an incredible thing happened. Instantly everyone started hearing the rumour:

"An Old Man is happy today, he doesn't complain about anything, smiles, and even his face is freshened up."

The whole village gathered together. The old man was asked:

Villager: What happened to you?

"Nothing special. Eighty years I've been chasing happiness, and it was useless. And then I decided to live without happiness and just enjoy life. That's why I'm happy now." – An Old Man

Moral: Don't chase happiness. Enjoy your life.

CHAPTER FOURTEEN

Ch : 14 The Foolish Donkey

- Ch : 14 The Foolish Donkey

A salt seller used to carry the salt bag on his donkey to the market every day.

On the way they had to cross a stream. One day the donkey suddenly tumbled down the stream and the salt bag also fell into the water. The salt dissolved in the water and hence the bag became very light to carry. The donkey was happy.

Then the donkey started to play the same trick every day.

The salt seller came to understand the trick and decided to teach a lesson to it. The next day he loaded a cotton bag on the donkey.

Again it played the same trick hoping that the cotton bag would be still become lighter.

But the dampened cotton became very heavy to carry and the donkey suffered. It learnt a lesson. It didn't play the trick anymore after that day, and the seller was happy.

Moral: Luck won't favor always.

CHAPTER FIFTEEN

Ch : 15 Having A Best Friend

- Ch : 15 Having A Best Friend

A story tells that two friends were walking through the desert. During some point of the journey they had an argument, and one friend slapped the other one in the face.

The one who got slapped was hurt, but without saying anything, wrote in the sand;

"Today my best friend slapped me in the face."

They kept on walking until they found an oasis, where they decided to take a bath. The one who had been slapped got stuck in the mire and started drowning, but the friend saved him. After he recovered from the near drowning, he wrote on a stone;

"Today my best friend saved my life."

The friend who had slapped and saved his best friend asked him."After I hurt you, you wrote in the sand and now, you write on a stone, why?"The other friend replied;

"When someone hurts us we should write it down in sand where winds of forgiveness can erase it away. But, when someone does something good for us, we must engrave it in stone where no wind can ever erase it."

Moral: Don't value the things you have in your life. But value who you have in your life.

CHAPTER SIXTEEN

Ch : 16 The Four Smart Students

- Ch : 16 The Four Smart Students

One night four college students were out partying late night and didn't study for the test which was scheduled for the next day. In the morning, they thought of a plan.

They made themselves look dirty with grease and dirt.

Then they went to the Dean and said they had gone out to a wedding last night and on their way back the tire of their car burst and they had to push the car all the way back. So they were in no condition to take the test.

The Dean thought for a minute and said they can have the re-test after 3 days. They thanked him and said they will be ready by that time.

On the third day, they appeared before the Dean. The Dean said that as this was a Special Condition Test, all four were required to sit in separate classrooms for the test. They all agreed as they had prepared well in the last 3 days.

The Test consisted of only 2 questions with the total of 100 Points:

1) Your Name? __________ (1 Points)

2) Which tire burst? __________ (99 Points)

Options – (a) Front Left (b) Front Right (c) Back Left (d) Back Right

Moral: Take responsibility or you will learn your lesson.

CHAPTER SEVENTEEN

Ch : 17 The Greedy Lion

- Ch : 17 The Greedy Lion

It was an incredibly hot day, and a lion was feeling very hungry.He came out of his den and searched here and there. He could find only a small hare. He caught the hare with some hesitation. “This hare can’t fill my stomach” thought the lion.

As the lion was about to kill the hare, a deer ran that way. The lion became greedy. He thought;

“Instead of eating this small hare, let me eat the big deer.”

He let the hare go and went behind the deer. But the deer had vanished into the forest. The lion now felt sorry for letting the hare off.

Moral: A bird in hand is worth two in the bush.

CHAPTER EIGHTEEN

Ch : 18 Two Friends & The Bear

- Ch : 18 Two Friends & The Bear

Vijay and Raju were friends. On a holiday they went walking into a forest, enjoying the beauty of nature. Suddenly they saw a bear coming at them. They became frightened.

Raju, who knew all about climbing trees, ran up to a tree and climbed up quickly. He didn't think of Vijay. Vijay had no idea how to climb the tree.

Vijay thought for a second. He'd heard animals don't prefer dead bodies, so he fell to the ground and held his breath. The bear sniffed him and thought he was dead. So, it went on its way.

Raju asked Vijay;

"What did the bear whisper into your ears?"

Vijay replied, "The bear asked me to keep away from friends like you" ...and went on his way.

Moral: A friend in need is a friend indeed.

CHAPTER NINETEEN

Ch : 19 The Struggles of Our Life

- Ch : 19 The Struggles of Our Life

Once upon a time a daughter complained to her father that her life was miserable and that she didn't know how she was going to make it.She was tired of fighting and struggling all the time. It seemed just as one problem was solved, another one soon followed.

Her father, a chef, took her to the kitchen. He filled three pots with water and placed each on a high fire.Once the three pots began to boil, he placed potatoes in one pot, eggs in the second pot and ground coffee beans in the third pot. He then let them sit and boil, without saying a word to his daughter.

The daughter, moaned and impatiently waited, wondering what he was doing. After twenty minutes he turned off the burners.He took the potatoes out of the pot and placed them in a bowl. He pulled the eggs out and placed them in a bowl. He then ladled the coffee out and placed it in a cup.

Turning to her, he asked. "Daughter, what do you see?"

"Potatoes, eggs and coffee," she hastily replied."Look closer" he said, "and touch the potatoes." She did and noted that they were soft.He then asked her to take an egg and break it. After pulling off the shell, she observed the hard-boiled egg.

Finally, he asked her to sip the coffee. Its rich aroma brought a smile to her face."Father, what does this mean?" she asked.He then explained that the potatoes, the eggs and coffee beans had each faced the same adversity-the boiling water. However, each one reacted differently. The potato went in strong, hard and unrelenting, but in boiling water, it became soft and weak.

The egg was fragile, with the thin outer shell protecting its liquid interior until it was put in the boiling water. Then the inside of the egg became hard.

However, the ground coffee beans were unique. After they were exposed to the boiling water, they changed the water and created something new."Which one are you?" he asked his daughter."When adversity knocks on your door, how do you respond? Are you a potato, an egg, or a coffee bean?"

Moral: In life, things happen around us, things happen to us, but the only thing that truly matters is how you choose to react to it and what you make out of it. Life is all about leaning, adopting and converting all the struggles that we experience into something positive.

CHAPTER TWENTY

Ch : 20 The Fox & The Grapes

- Ch : 20 The Fox & The Grapes

One afternoon a fox was walking through the forest and spotted a bunch of grapes hanging from over a lofty branch.

"Just the thing to quench my thirst," he thought.

Taking a few steps back, the fox jumped and just missed the hanging grapes. Again the fox took a few paces back and tried to reach them but still failed.

Finally, giving up, the fox turned up his nose and said, "They're probably sour anyway," and proceeded to walk away.

Moral: It's easy to despise what you can't have.

CHAPTER TWENTY-ONE

Ch : 21 The Lion & The Poor Slave

- Ch : 21 The Lion & The Poor Slave

A slave, ill-treated by his master, runs away to the forest. There he comes across a lion in pain because of a thorn in his paw. The slave bravely goes forward and removes the thorn gently.

The lion without hurting him goes away.

Some days later, the slave's master comes hunting to the forest and catches many animals and cages them. The slave is spotted by the masters' men who catch him and bring him to the cruel master.

The master asks for the slave to be thrown into the lion's cage.The slave is awaiting his death in the cage when he realizes that it is the same lion that he had helped. The slave rescued the lion and all other caged animals.

Moral: One should help others in need, we get the rewards of our helpful acts in return.

CHAPTER TWENTY-TWO

Ch : 22 Shark Bait

- Ch : 22 Shark Bait

A marine biologist put a shark into a big tank at the time of a research experiment. Followed by that, he released some tiny bait fishes into it.

As expected, the shark didn't wait to attack those fishes and ate them. Later, a clear fiberglass was inserted into the tank which partitioned the tank into two and the shark remained in one side.

A similar set of bait fish was sent to the other side of the tank like before. And the shark attempted to attack those fishes but failed by hitting on the fiberglass.

The shark attempted for several days until it gave up. Later, the biologist removed the glass from the tank but the shark didn't try to attack the small fishes.the shark always continues to see a false barrier in the tank and stopped his attempts.

Moral: It is quite common for many people to give up after many setbacks and failures. The story is an example for keep trying always and to never give up despite multiple failures.

CHAPTER TWENTY-THREE

Ch : 23 Struggles develop strength

- Ch : 23 Struggles develop strength

One day a man was passing by a garden when he saw a butterfly cocoon which was about to get open.

He saw a small opening on it and watched the several hours of struggles the butterfly came through to get the body out of it. After many hours, it seemed that the butterfly stopped trying as there was no progress.

He thought to help the butterfly by cutting the cocoon with a scissor. So the butterfly came out easily but the wings were shriveled and the body was tiny and withered.Unfortunately, the butterfly was not able to take flight and spend the rest of life crawling with a wounded body.

Moral: This is nature's way of telling the importance of struggles in life. Sometimes, different kinds of struggles are needed in life to make you stronger in the future. Never feel disappointed in life and stop trying when life offers you struggles but keep on fighting until you see success.

CHAPTER TWENTY-FOUR

Ch : 24 Seeing opportunity in obstacles

- Ch : 24 Seeing opportunity in obstacles

Once there was a king who was curious but wealthy. He decided to test his fellow people to know who has a got a good attitude in life and who would spare some time for country's progress.

He placed a huge boulder right at the middle of the road and hid in a nearby place to see if anyone would make an attempt to move it off.

He saw some wealthy merchants and courtiers passing by the road. None of them made any attempt to move it off but simply walked away while some others blamed the king for not maintaining roads.

Later, a peasant came the way with a load of vegetables and saw the boulder. He kept his load down and tried to move the boulder away. After strenuous effort, he succeeded in moving it away. He saw a purse lying in the place of the boulder.

It contained many gold coins and a note from the king which read 'this is the reward for the person who moves the boulder away'.

Moral: It is quite common for people to run away from problems and obstacles. But the story clearly shows the importance of seeing an opportunity in every obstacle which might improve our condition. Invest some time to remove obstacles on your way and experience many unseen presences.

CHAPTER TWENTY-FIVE

Ch : 25 Shake off problems

- Ch : 25 Shake off problems

A man and his donkey were on the way to grazing while the donkey fell into a huge pit. The man was shaken and tried hard to pull off his favorite donkey up to the ground.

Despite his strenuous attempts, he failed to bring the donkey back. But he can't leave the donkey to starve and die with pain for days.

So he decided to bury him alive and make his death smoother. So he started pouring soil over the donkey in the pit. When he poured the soil, the donkey felt the load and shakes it off and he steps on it.He does the same every time when the soil was poured on his body. In the end, he reached the ground level and easily walked away to graze in the green pastures.

Moral: Don't choose to live with your problem. Just shake off your problems and stand on it and step up in life after learning from them. Every bad experience is a new learning. So get the positives out of it and work towards your goals.

CHAPTER TWENTY-SIX

Ch : 26 Let go of your stresses

- Ch : 26 Let go of your stresses

A psychology professor entered the classroom with half a glass of water in his hand. The students expected the old common question "was it half empty or half full?" But to the surprise, he asked them "How heavy is this glass of water?"

The answers given by the students ranged from 7 oz. To 25 oz. But the professor replied that the actual weight of the glass with water doesn't always matter but how long you hold the glass is what matters.

If you hold the glass for a minute, you won't feel much weight. But if you hold for 10 minutes, you will feel a little more weight and it gets heavier for you with hours.

If you hold it for the entire day, then your hands would go numb and pain. Similar is the case when you carry stress with you. If you think about it for a while and leave it, then there is no problem but if you think about it for hours, it starts becoming a problem and it becomes worse if you sleep with it.

Moral: You should learn to let go of your stresses and never sleep with it. If you can do something about it, just do it. In the other case, just leave it and work towards your goals or else it just kills your productivity.

CHAPTER TWENTY-SEVEN

Ch : 27 Value yourself

- Ch : 27 Value yourself

A speaker started off his seminar by showing a $20 to the public. He asked the people "who wants this?" There was no surprise to see that all of them lifted their hands. He offered to give the money to one of them but insisted that he will do something to it.

He crumpled the paper money and showed it again to the crowd and repeated the question. Still, everyone raised the hands. He then put the money into the ground and stepped on it and then raised it again and offered it to the public.

The people gathered there still showed interest to take that money despite seeing how dirty the note was. He told the public" No matter what I did to this money, you all still wanted this.You all went in favor of my offer just because the value of the money never decreased despite what all I did to it. Similarly, value yourself despite the painful conditions or failures"

Moral: Believe in yourself and work hard to achieve success. Value yourself irrespective of the failures or obstacles and don't degrade yourself just because of the temporary setbacks.

CHAPTER TWENTY-EIGHT

Ch : 28 Sharpen your 'axe'

- Ch : 28 Sharpen your 'axe'

There was a newly joined woodcutter and the king was really impressed by his dedication towards his work. Out of encouragement, he started giving his best in work and cut 18 trees in the first month and the king was glad.

The next month he put in the same effort but could cut only 15 trees. And the third month, he still tried his best but could cut only 12 trees. The king visited him the third month and talked about his decrease in productivity.

He explained that he might have lost his strength or got too old to do the work. The king asked him "when was the last time you sharpened your ax?" To the surprise, he has not even done it once in the last three months. That was the only reason why he couldn't cut more trees.

Moral: It is good that you put in a lot of effort and hard work to work towards your goals. But you should balance your life priorities and invest time with your family and save some time to relax which would boost up your productivity.

These are just a few among the many motivational stories that guide students to work hard on many aspects of life and grow successful. Such inspirational stories can help students to keep moral values in life despite whatever life offers them.

CHAPTER TWENTY-NINE

Ch : 29 Laziness won't get you anywhere

- Ch : 29 Laziness won't get you anywhere

In ancient times, a king had his men place a boulder on a roadway. He then hid in the bushes, and watched to see if anyone would move the boulder out of the way. Some of the king's wealthiest merchants and courtiers passed by and simply walked around it.

Many people blamed the King for not keeping the roads clear, but none of them did anything about getting the stone removed.

One day, a peasant came along carrying vegetables. Upon approaching the boulder, the peasant laid down his burden and tried to push the stone out of the way. After much pushing and straining, he finally managed.

After the peasant went back to pick up his vegetables, he noticed a purse lying in the road where the boulder had been. The purse contained many gold coins and note from the King explain that the gold was for the person who removed the boulder from the road.

CHAPTER THIRTY

Ch : 30 Don't say something you regret out of anger

- Ch : 30 Don’t say something you regret out of anger

There once was a little boy who had a very bad temper. His father decided to hand him a bag of nails and said that every time the boy lost his temper, he had to hammer a nail into the fence.

On the first day, the boy hammered 37 nails into that fence.

The boy gradually began to control his temper over the next few weeks, and the number of nails he was hammering into the fence slowly decreased. He discovered it was easier to control his temper than to hammer those nails into the fence.

Finally, the day came when the boy didn’t lose his temper at all. He told his father the news and the father suggested that the boy should now pull out a nail every day he kept his temper under control.

The days passed and the young boy was finally able to tell his father that all the nails were gone. The father took his son by the hand and led him to the fence.

‘You have done well, my son, but look at the holes in the fence. The fence will never be the same. When you say things in anger, they leave a scar just like this one. You can put a knife in a man and draw it out. It won’t matter how many times you say I’m sorry, the wound is still there.'

CHAPTER THIRTY-ONE

Ch : 31 Damaged souls still have worth

- Ch : 31 Damaged souls still have worth

A shop owner placed a sign above his door that said: 'Puppies For Sale.'

Signs like this always have a way of attracting young children, and to no surprise, a boy saw the sign and approached the owner; 'How much are you going to sell the puppies for?' he asked.The store owner replied, 'Anywhere from $30 to $50.'The little boy pulled out some change from his pocket. 'I have $2.37,' he said. 'Can I please look at them?'

The shop owner smiled and whistled. Out of the kennel came Lady, who ran down the aisle of his shop followed by five teeny, tiny balls of fur.

One puppy was lagging considerably behind. Immediately the little boy singled out the lagging, limping puppy and said, 'What's wrong with that little dog?'

The shop owner explained that the veterinarian had examined the little puppy and had discovered it didn't have a hip socket. It would always limp. It would always be lame.The little boy became excited. 'That is the puppy that I want to buy.'The shop owner said, 'No, you don't want to buy that little dog. If you really want him, I'll just give him to you.'

The little boy got quite upset. He looked straight into the store owner's eyes, pointing his finger, and said;

'I don't want you to give him to me. That little dog is worth every bit as much as all the other dogs and I'll pay full price. In fact, I'll give you $2.37 now, and 50 cents a month until I have him paid for.'

The shop owner countered, 'You really don't want to buy this little dog. He is never going to be able to run and jump and play with you like the other puppies.'

To his surprise, the little boy reached down and rolled up his pant leg to reveal a badly twisted, crippled left leg supported by a big metal brace. He looked up at the shop owner and softly replied, 'Well, I don't run so well myself, and the little puppy will need someone who understands!

CHAPTER THIRTY-TWO

Ch : 32 Never let one failure from the past hold you back in the future

- Ch : 32 Never let one failure from the past hold you back in the future

As a man was passing the elephants, he suddenly stopped, confused by the fact that these huge creatures were being held by only a small rope tied to their front leg. No chains, no cages. It was obvious that the elephants could, at anytime, break away from their bonds but for some reason, they did not.

He saw a trainer nearby and asked why these animals just stood there and made no attempt to get away. 'Well,' trainer said, 'when they are very young and much smaller we use the same size rope to tie them and, at that age, it's enough to hold them. As they grow up, they are conditioned to believe they cannot break away. They believe the rope can still hold them, so they never try to break free.'

The man was amazed. These animals could at any time break free from their bonds but because they believed they couldn't, they were stuck right where they were.

The End .....

Thank You So Much Message

For Your Supported & For Your Loves Thank You So Much. Have A Greatest Day Of Your. If I am successful today, because of my father, if he lived today, he would have been very happy, he will always and always be with me.

Printed by Libri Plureos GmbH in Hamburg,
Germany